Living a Productive Life

Tadhg O'Flaherty

Copyright © 2016 by Tadhg O'Flaherty

All Rights Reserved. No part of this publication may be reproduced, distributed, or transmitted in any form or by any means, including photocopying, recording, or other electronic or mechanical methods, without the prior written permission of the author, except in the case of brief quotations embodied in critical reviews and certain other noncommercial uses permitted by copyright law.

This document provides exact and reliable information with regards to the topic covered. The publication is sold with the understanding that the author is not required to render accounting, officially permitted, or otherwise, qualified services. If further advice is required, legal or professional, a practised individual in the required profession should be consulted.

The information contained in this book is intended for educational purposes only and is not for diagnosis, prescription or treatment of any health disorder whatsoever. The productivity techniques described within are potentially dangerous and should not be performed without first consulting with a competent health care or legal professional and/or a professional within the respective field. By following the various techniques described in this book you do so at your own risk.

The author will not be held liable for any reparation, damages, or monetary loss due to the use or misuse of the material contained within. The information within is offered for informational purposes only and is without contract or any type of guarantee.

ISBN-13: 978-1-52052-682-9

To the hopelessly stressed-out and over-worked.

Because you deserve a break.

Table of Contents

Introduction 1

What is Your Long-Term Goal? 3

    Make a Plan 4

    Prioritise 5

    Categorise and Sub-Categorise 6

    Anticipate Obstacles 8

Stress 9

    Don't Dwell on Failure 14

The Myth of Motivation 18

Declutter 22

    Removing Distractions 26

Nourishment 29

    Drink more water 30

    Exercise 32

    Learning 34

    Social Connections 37

Embrace Happiness 40

    Destroy Negativity 42

    Gratitude 44

    Focus and Meditation 47

    Daydream 49

- Cultivate Childlike Curiosity 51
- See it as Already Finished 52
- The Importance of Sleep 55
  - The Resting Paradox 58
  - Slow Down and Relax 61
- Are You Rich or Wealthy? 63
  - Keeping up with the Jones's 65
- Conclusion 68

Introduction

"Concentrate all your thoughts upon the work in hand. The sun's rays do not burn until brought to a focus."
Alexander Graham Bell (1847-1922)

In today's hectic world where everything needs to be done right away, people have a tendency to overwork themselves to the point where nothing gets done properly. This, in turn, creates a dangerous spiral of mistakes, procrastination, stress, sleep deprivation and psychological disorders such as anxiety or depression.

In order to alleviate this progressive spiral, it is important that you become far more productive and learn how to focus your mind properly on the most important tasks.

It doesn't matter how difficult these tasks are or how many things you need to accomplish on a daily basis. The most important thing to realise is that the struggle to achieve these things does not need to be a struggle at all.

Many people will take on far too much work and think that the only way to get it all done is to deprive themselves of valuable sleep or become a workaholic in order to get everything finished, however, stepping back from tasks is invaluable when trying to become more productive at doing those tasks.

By utilising the techniques presented in this book you will find you're your productivity rates can, and will, improve dramatically and ultimately result in a far better quality of life.

What is Your Long-Term Goal?

"Do the hard jobs first. The easy jobs will take care of themselves."
Dale Carnegie (1888-1955)

Before you can possibly become more productive you need to have a clear image of what it is you are trying to achieve. Without this, you will not have a goal to reach for and will aimlessly carry out your daily tasks which will ultimately lead you nowhere.

Is your ultimate goal to become the CEO of a company or to record a song or to write a book? Take some time to sit down and clearly identify where you want to be. You don't need to try and figure out how to get there, all you need to do is identify that final and ultimate goal. Got this image in mind? Great ... now write it out on paper, or type it in detail. Frame this piece of paper and hang it on the wall in your home office or in another prominent area where you will see it regularly. This is no different to a company printing its business plan and hanging it in the reception area of their building.

Make a Plan

Now that you have figured out your long-term goal it is time to list the steps necessary in order to achieve that goal. You don't need to go into great detail, just a few bullet points will do.

Try to list those things that are major pointers on the road to achieving your goal. For example, if you want to be the CEO of your own company you will need to learn about what paperwork is necessary in your country to register a limited company, where and how to secure a premises, the equipment necessary to create or sell your product and how to source appropriate employees.

It doesn't need to be as big as the creation of your own company; it could be as simple as planning out your day at work in advance.

Prioritise

What is the most vital task that must be performed today in order to bring you slightly closer to your goal? Tackle that issue first, before anything else. If you begin your day by procrastinating on the vital tasks you will be sending a strong and powerful message into the Universe that you are not serious about your long-term goal and it will respond accordingly by denying you that great goal you are trying to achieve.

If however, you tackle the priority task head-on the Universe will respond by making things a little bit easier for you each day and open up opportunities where there once was none.

You may find that the priority task takes all day to finish and you are left with a long list of more insignificant tasks that build up as the days go on. It is best to ignore these tasks as they are not vital. As you ignore these smaller tasks you will eventually be in a position where the priority takes a fraction of the time it used to and tackling those minor tasks becomes possible.

Categorise and Sub-Categorise

Now that you know exactly what tasks are a priority and are working on them accordingly it is time to make a plan for those minor tasks. As minor as they may be they will still have an order of priority.

List down **all** the tasks that you need to perform today. Include everything, not just work related things. Do you need to wash your clothes today or clean the kitchen? List those type of personal tasks alongside your work related ones.

That daily priority task should now be listed at the top in big bold writing. After that you could have the heading "*household*" and sub-categorise all related tasks under that, such as cleaning the kitchen.

Once the list is complete it is time to attach a number beside each heading. Think very carefully about this one as things like the household tasks should really be listed last as you can't do them while at work.

By categorising your work in such a logical order you will be giving yourself a great sense of achievement as you cross off each one as it is completed. As you mark each one as done take a minute to acknowledge that the completion of this task is bringing you closer to your life-long goal, no matter how insignificant that task may seem.

Anticipate Obstacles

It is very easy to make a plan that accounts for each and every minute of your day, but such a plan gets completely off-track with something as simple as going for a poop. How long did that take you, 5 or 10 minutes? How are you going to catch up with your unbelievably tight schedule?

Not only do you need to account for the normal everyday inconveniences to your schedule but you must also factor in the possibility of obstacles interfering with your work. Always make sure that each item on your schedule has added time for when things go wrong.

By having this extra time factored into your schedule you will also create a scenario where most tasks will be completed ahead of schedule which in turn will give you a great boost in mood and a sense of accomplishment.

Stress

"The greatest weapon against stress is our ability to choose one thought over another."
William James (1842-1910)

You know those nagging little life issues that are building up in your mind every day? The kind of things that usually revolve around your finances, family life, the sheer mountain of work on your desk that was supposed to be finished last month, the broken down car and the fridge that stopped working two days ago. These things, taken individually, will cause you to experience a little bit of stress. Taken collectively they are causing such a build-up of stress in your system that they are literally killing you. Years are being stripped off your lifespan unnecessarily.

I want to be very clear on this next point. Regardless of your current belief system when it comes to stress or the build-up of stress ... *"It only exists in your mind and only exists because you **want** it to exist."* Think about it, when the car broke down it didn't extend some probe from the dashboard that entered your ear and reached into your brain to implant some stress about the situation, you were the one that cultivated the thoughts that lead you to experience stress.

Constantly experiencing stress (which only exists in your mind) will lead to the following real world symptoms:

- Racing and broken thoughts
- Severe disorganisation
- Poor judgement
- Forgetfulness
- Being unable to focus on simple tasks
- Constant negative mood
- Nervous behaviour
- Increased consumption of drugs or alcohol
- Procrastination
- Loss of appetite

If you do not get control of your stress it will lead you to experience chronic stress which in turn will lead to very serious health issues down the line.

These include:

- Depression
- Eating disorder
- Gastrointestinal issues
- Hair loss
- Sexual dysfunction or loss of sexual desire
- Heart disease
- High blood pressure
- Stroke

While stress will always be present in our everyday lives it is vital to change how you react to moments of stress. One way of doing this is to cultivate a new belief system where you see stressful situations as things that are actively steering you towards a better outcome in the long-run.

For example, if the car keeps breaking down, instead of allowing this situation to cause negative thoughts you should close your eyes and count very slowly to 10. While you are counting, in your mind, take long deep breaths. When you reach 10, keep your eyes closed and continue taking deep breaths. Now empty your mind of all thoughts and only concentrate on your breathing, nothing exists in this world, only your breathing. Do this for about 10 minutes and open your eyes. If you have never done such an exercise before then congratulations, you have just done some meditation for the first time in your life.

While you are standing at the side of the road, waiting for the recovery vehicle I want you to come up with some positive reasons why the Universe would cause your car to break down today. Maybe you have avoided certain death in a crash that is happening 20km (12.5 miles) away. Maybe you are due something nice, like a brand new car? Think about how great it would be to drive that new car. Concentrate on how smooth the drive would be. If you concentrate on this positive aspect for long enough you will literally begin to smell that beautiful new car smell.

Regardless of the stressful situation you are facing there is always a positive aspect that you **must** find.

Another great way to eliminate stress is to let it all go at the end of the day. Do this when you are lying in bed and about to drift off to sleep. Imagine each stressful situation that you have experienced during the day as being a shovelful of dirt that you are putting into a small wicker basket. Each stressful moment is its own shovel of dirt and each moment belongs in its own basket. When you are finished imagine that you unpack some balloons and tie these to the wicker baskets. This is such an un-stressful exercise that you don't even need to blow up the balloons yourself, you have a large container of helium beside you and all you need to do is turn a handle to fill the balloons. As each balloon fills watch it slowly drift into the sky. When the last balloon begins to float away, realise that you can't even see the previous balloons anymore, they are well gone. Now those balloons and the baskets of stress that they carry are the Universes problem to deal with, you are free to drift off to sleep without a care in the world.

Don't Dwell on Failure

Did you know that the most successful, productive and richest people on this planet fail on a daily basis? How they deal with failure sets them apart from the rest of us. Most people will give up at the first hurdle, even if they are pursuing a lifelong dream. Failure is part and parcel of human existence and is designed to teach us some lesson. The lesson could be as simple as how not to do something.

The only way to become an expert at anything is to constantly persevere no matter what obstacles get in your way. If you do something for long enough you are guaranteed to experience failure. Each failure that you experience will teach you a lesson, so when you persevere with your project you will know what not to do. Each small failure will eventually lead to you perfecting whatever you are trying to achieve.

When you encounter a failure it is vital that you stop what you are doing and search your mind for the positive in this bad situation. It is there, you just need to look for it. Don't continue until you have found that one positive aspect and acknowledge that this does not mean that you should give up completely.

A series of failures that are happening every few minutes is the Universes way of telling you to stop for the day and return tomorrow. This one might be well worth noting as you may find that by stopping for the day and going somewhere else you may encounter someone who has experienced the same failures who can guide you in the right direction or give you some insight that may make you come to the solution yourself.

If you encounter a complete block, where you can't proceed without first getting an answer to what you are stuck on, it is best if you abandon what you are doing, close your eyes and loudly declare (in your own mind), "Universe, I want the answer to ..." and add whatever it is you are stuck on. Now walk away from your desk, or wherever you are working, and believe that you have found the answer. Think thoughts of what you will be doing now that you have the answer. Say if your project requires steps A, B and C but you are stuck on B. You should imagine now that you are performing step C and it should feel great.

The answer you are looking for will be delivered to you in no time. You just need to believe with all of your mighty powers.

The Myth of Motivation

"Every time you come in yelling that God damn "Rise and Shine!" "Rise and Shine!" I say to myself, "How lucky dead people are!"
Tennessee Williams (1911-1983)

Motivation is everywhere these days. We are being constantly bombarded with motivational videos, speeches and websites that teach you how to get motivated. But what exactly will motivation achieve? In the end, it will be more of a hindrance than a help, as motivation is a fleeting thing that will come crashing down at some stage. The best analogy to use when talking about motivation is the effects of taking drugs. I will use LSD in this example as it comes very close to mimicking the effects of motivation.

LSD (Lysergic Acid Diethylamide), better known as *"acid"* is a psychedelic drug that causes the user to experience an altered awareness and deliver sensations and images to their brain that simply doesn't exist in reality. While motivation will not alter your awareness or cause you to have hallucinations it can be compared to LSD in the way it begins to work, how long it last for and the after effects.

When you first take LSD nothing significant will happen for approximately 20 minutes, at which time you will get very giddy and laugh at anything and everything. When you want to get motivated you will spend some time trying to boost your mood and psyche yourself up for the task ahead of you. Maybe you will do this in the morning as you get ready for work. Maybe this will extend to preparing breakfast and even in the car on the way to work. Just like LSD, it might take you 20 minutes to get yourself into a motivated mood.

For the next 12 hours, you will be high on the effects of LSD. Motivation might even last 12 hours also, especially if you are working a 12-hour shift at work, on some vitally important project or proposal that **must** be ready for tomorrow morning. This length of motivation is great and will aid you greatly in achieving your goal for the day but the biggest problem is what happens after those 12 hours.

After 12 hours the effects of LSD and motivation will wear off and you will find yourself in a state of complete exhaustion where nothing is possible, even rest becomes difficult. You will not be able to sit still or be able to accomplish much at this stage because your body has been operating at its fullest for an extended period of time. This come-down stage can last as long as the motivation itself, up to 12 hours.

A far better solution is to **not** motivate yourself to complete a task, or get up and go to work, or complete that project. Instead, cultivate the habit of just dragging yourself out of bed and going to work. Over time you will perfect this to such an extent that your body, and brain, will simply accept the fact that you need to get up at a certain time and work for a certain length of time. This is far better in the long-run because motivation will only leave you drained and exhausted and cannot be sustained for long periods of time or over many days, weeks, or months.

Declutter

"Out of clutter, find simplicity."
Albert Einstein (1879-1955)

Take a quick look around your house, making sure to visit every room. While you're at it open some wardrobes and drawers. Does the place seem like a mess to you? If it does then it's simply a culmination of acquiring far too many items, most of which you no longer need or use.

I want you to spend some time to go through all of your possessions with a view to performing the biggest declutter ever. Regardless of how busy you are, this declutter is vital for boosting your overall productivity levels because all of those unorganised things, or unfinished projects or discarded hobbies are constantly nagging at your subconscious mind. Think of this in terms of a computer; all of that clutter can be thought of as a bunch of programs running in the background that is constantly slowing down your system. Most of these programs can be safely removed because they are no longer needed. This frees up the CPU from these needless tasks and as a result, it will perform far better and focus almost all of its computational power on the real tasks that it needs to perform.

Another damaging consequence of having all of this clutter nagging at your subconscious is that it will dramatically affect your ability to sleep and the quality of any sleep that you do get. Free your mind of clutter by freeing your reality of clutter.

The best way to tackle any decluttering is to simply get it over with as fast as possible. You will not be decluttering your desk or a single room ... you will be decluttering your entire house in one foul swoop.

I know this can be a daunting task but there are some techniques that will make this job run quickly and smoothly. Let's say that you are starting in the kitchen. Take every single item and pile it up on the kitchen table. Empty every drawer and every cupboard. Have you piled everything onto the table? Great, now if you want to eat dinner later you better get those items sorted out first.

To make things easier you can deal with large collections of items that you can instantly identify as rubbish such as pizza boxes or newspapers. Bring these out to the bin immediately and dispose of them. Now grab 4 very large boxes and mark them:

- Trash
- Giveaway
- Sell
- Put away

Take any random item from the pile of things on your kitchen table and decide which container it belongs in. The decision-making process should take no more than 3 seconds per item. If you find that it takes a lot longer than 3 seconds to decide, or that you simply can't decide and want to keep everything so you put it all in the put away box than you may have a problem with hoarding. If this is the case you will need to seek professional help to deal with your hoarding issue. There will be items that you can't make a decision about but this should constitute a tiny pile of items compared to the amount that was previously in that room.

As soon as the boxes are full you should empty them immediately. Throw out the items in the **trash** box and store the items in the **put away** box. Put the contents of the **give-away** box in your car or in a pile by the front door. At the end of today, you will take these items to the charity shop or to the friend or family member that you are giving them to. Do not neglect this pile of stuff; get it out of your house as soon as possible. The items in the sell box should be carefully piled in a corner of one room and dealt with once the entire house has been fully decluttered.

Removing Distractions

The clutter in your home is not the only thing that is causing disruption in your subconscious mind. Plenty of other things are still there causing trouble. Let's take a close look at your computer, either at home or at work. How does the Desktop look? Are there icons scattered all over the place or are they organised? If the Desktop is all over the place you will need to clean it up. Either create folders to hold multiple icons or download a dock that can organise the icons for you. Check all of the installed software to ensure you really need each program. If there are any that can be safely uninstalled go ahead and get rid of them.

You know those 12,568 emails that are clogging your inbox? We need to deal with these also. This one can be tackled in a similar way to removing the clutter in your house. Create 3 folders marked:

- Reply to
- Read
- Store

Just like in your home you can take a quick look for any series of emails that can be deleted in bulk, these will be things like subscriber newsletters that you don't have an interest in anymore. Perform a mass delete on all such newsletters.

Next, go through each email and quickly scan the contents to determine if you need to reply, read it more thoroughly or store it. Don't reply to any emails just yet, just move them to the appropriate folder as you can deal with these later. For any emails that you want to keep you can create new folders that relate to the specific subject of the emails in your **store** folder and organise these as needed.

When you have moved or deleted **all** emails in your inbox you can reply to the ones that require your attention and then store these emails in their appropriate folders or delete them. While you're at it go ahead and delete the contents of your **Trash (Deleted Items)** folder if these are no longer needed. Now sit back and bask in your shiny, bright and empty inbox ... oh wait, you're not finished just yet. If you have bookmarks in your internet browser you need to deal with this clutter also. Just like your inbox, you can create folders for storing important bookmarks and mass delete the ones you no longer need.

Don't neglect these steps as they will go a long way to freeing up your subconscious for the important tasks that you need to perform, and you will sleep much better, which will boost your productivity levels by leaps and bounds.

Nourishment

"Let food be thy medicine and medicine be thy food."
Hippocrates (c. 460 – 370 BC)

Healthy body, healthy mind. This statement is used on a nearly constant basis. But what does that really mean? It means exactly what it says. If you keep your body healthy and fed with the correct nutrition you will be rewarded with a sharp and focused mind.

It is very easy in today's hectic work life to neglect healthy meals and opt instead for the convenience of fast food and trash from vending machines. It is vital that you make healthy food your only source of nourishment from Monday to Saturday. You can eat whatever you like on Sunday, that's your day off.

Stay clear of processed foods wherever possible and rid your mind of the idea that *"diet"* foods are healthy, they are not. Whenever you see *"diet"* on a product replace this word with the phrase *"chemical shit-storm"*. The regular version of a diet product will always be better and healthier. At the same time, if that product does have a diet version than that product itself is almost always an unhealthy food and should be avoided.

Drink more water

Most people will spend their working day consuming large quantities of coffee and soft drinks. While these drinks will give you a small quantity of water they will inevitably cause you to become more dehydrated. While teas and coffee are perfectly okay, soft drinks must be removed from your existence between Monday and Saturday as these drinks will cause you serious illness if consumed in great quantities over an extended period of time. You should be drinking 2 litres (4.3 pints) of water per day in order to keep yourself adequately hydrated.

Don't get overzealous as drinking too much water will kill you. When you drink too much water your kidneys will become overwhelmed which will result in a condition known as hyponatremia. The symptoms of hyponatremia include:

- Feeling light headed
- Nausea
- Weight gain
- Headaches
- Vomiting
- Confusion
- Agitation
- Delirium
- Seizures
- Coma

You will lose water on a daily basis simply by being alive. Activities such as breathing, sweating, urinating and even pooping will cause you to lose water and this needs to be replenished in order to maintain a healthy level of reserves in your system.

Exercise

It may sound very counterintuitive that you should be doing physical exercise. After all, you are trying to become more productive. Surely a daily exercise regime will only take time away from your already busy schedule? Before you abandon this section, ask yourself this question ... how productive do you become when you spend a few days in bed with the flu?

You should formulate an exercise plan that spans, at the minimum 5 days (Monday to Friday) and at the maximum 6 days (Monday to Saturday). It is vital that you take at least one day off per week. The physical exercise that you choose should be something you enjoy doing such as jogging, weight lifting, cycling or a combination.

The minimum amount of physical activity per day should be 1 hour and this should be a time where you really work out. No slacking off or taking it easy.

Lying in the Jacuzzi at the gym for 1 hour is **not** physical exercise; it is just a giant waste of your valuable time. By the time you return home from your exercise you should be covered from head-to-toe in sweat and feel exhausted. By the time you get out of the shower you will feel amazing and believe that you can conquer any challenge.

When you exercise, your brain will release endorphins which are the feel good drug that is responsible for making us feel happy. Strangely this release of endorphins is a result of the primitive part of your brain interpreting your strenuous physical exercise as a bid to escape some unknown vicious creature that may kill and eat you. The only reason that endorphins are released at this time is to block out pain and put your mind into a state of euphoria. By doing this the brain is preparing itself for the moment when this unseen creature catches up with you and eats you. The brain does not want to face such a terrible thing so will put itself into a state where it can comfortably face the inevitable.

In our relatively safe world, this release of endorphins will leave you feeling far more happy and in a general state of well-being. While the exercise itself should completely exhaust you, the endorphin buzz will ensure that by the time you are finished and have a shower you will be feeling fantastic.

Don't neglect your daily exercise. Your body and brain will reward you very handsomely for taking care of your overall health and physique.

Learning

Your brain needs to be constantly stimulated. It is the vital nourishment that most people neglect. Your brain can easily become stagnant and bored while going through the same monotonous existence that everyone seems to be getting themselves into these days.

By learning new things on a constant basis it will also encourage your brain to focus on tasks and projects that must be completed on a daily basis. As your brain does not want to be experiencing the monotony it will literally force itself to get these horrible tasks over and done with as fast as possible in order to get involved in more interesting learning activities.

In the evenings when your work day is over, instead of watching mind-numbing shows on TV until you fall into bed feeling far more exhausted than rested (even though you spent the evening sitting on the couch!), it is far better for your brain and overall mood if you engage in activities that stimulate your mind to do what it does best ... learning.

How many languages do you know? Why not learn a new one. Is there a country that you've always wanted to visit but felt that you couldn't because you don't know the local language? Great, then get actively involved in perfecting that language so you can visit this country and see all those sites that you have always dreamed about seeing. Don't ever let something hold you back from fulfilling your dreams.

By actively engaging your brain on learning new things every day you will also make yourself smarter and faster in your monotonous daily routine. Once you get into the habit of spending the evenings learning something new you will actively feel excited and exhilarated at the end of each working day to get home and study.

In case you don't know already, school is a complete waste of time. Most of the greatest inventions and scientific discoveries were not made by academics but were made by people who dropped out of school to pursue their dreams. Learning something for yourself, rather than someone forcing it down your throat, is far easier and you will learn a lot more in a far shorter space of time.

What are the things that you have always wondered about? Go ahead and learn about them. That laptop in front of you contains the entire world's knowledge. Make use of it.

Social Connections

As human beings we rely on human interaction, in fact, we crave it. Did you know that social isolation kills more people worldwide than obesity? Some of the symptoms of chronic loneliness include:

- Sleeplessness
- Paranoia
- Panic attacks
- Impaired immune response
- Type II diabetes
- Heart disease

- Premature death

Admitting to yourself that you are lonely is as easy as a drug addict coming to the revelation that they need and will accept help. Sit down and close your eyes. Think about how many friends you have (human friends, not internet based anonymous faces). Go through each one in your mind and try to recall the last time you met them in person. If this is difficult to figure out then you need to meet-up with them ASAP.

If you don't get enough social interaction you are doing yourself a terrible injustice and this **must** be corrected ... today. You may think that the large amount of interactions you have on a daily basis through internet based social networks is more than enough but you are very wrong. What you require is the presence of other human beings, not a computer screen.

Some of the easiest interactions are things like enjoying a coffee with a work colleague or close friend. Phone your friends and make sure that they meet you on the weekend for a coffee. One hour per week of such interaction will make all the difference. If you don't have any friends of close associates, and generally spend all of your time working, **you need to stop this behaviour immediately**. Get yourself out-and-about and meet new people. Go for walks in the park or visit nearby elderly people (they are most likely in a far more isolated condition than you are).

A great way to formulate new social interactions is by volunteering for a local charity, civil defence organisation or other group that meet on a regular basis. Cultivate new friendships and engage in these as much as possible.

Let's face it, you can't possibly be more productive in life if that life isn't going to last very long.

Embrace Happiness

"For every minute you are angry you lose sixty seconds of happiness."
Ralph Waldo Emerson (1803-1882)

If you spend your life being a negative Nancy than you are doing yourself a very bad disservice as your negativity will not only impact on those around you but will bring about a situation where the Universe will give you more and more reasons to be negative. In other words, more and more bad things will happen to you. This, in turn, will have a dramatic impact on your productivity levels as nothing will go right for you and delays will creep into your work.

A far better approach to life is to always and only concentrate your efforts towards positivity. If you are a bit of a negative Nancy or moaning Michael I want you to stop whatever you are doing and find a mirror. Take a good look at yourself and smile. This should be a big cheesy ear-to-ear grin and maintain this for 10 minutes. It's ok to stop every few minutes to rest those facial muscles but only rest for a few seconds.

Did you know that the human brain cannot distinguish properly if you are sad or happy and can be easily tricked into believing it is in one state or the other? By smiling at yourself in the mirror your brain will take the sensory input from your eyes and see that you are smiling. This will trigger a process in the brain where, if it sees you smiling then you must be happy, so it will respond by making you feel happy. It does this through the release of certain chemicals associated with happiness.

When you embrace happiness you will notice dramatic decreases in negatively impacting things such as stress and dramatic increases in positively impacting things such as:

- Lower risk for certain cancers
- Lower risk for diabetes
- Fewer instances of colds and flu
- Dramatic decrease in your chances of becoming depressed
- More stable anxiety levels
- Better sleep
- Developing a lust for life

An overall increase in your happiness levels will bring about a series of physical and psychological changes that result in you being far more productive and focused on important tasks. Happiness is so important to our existence that it should be developed into a vaccination, seeing as they are mandatory when you are young.

Destroy Negativity

In the drive to be more productive in any aspect of your life, negativity will be the ultimate enemy that must be defeated at all costs. It will seem to many that this will be a losing battle but did you know that you have the capacity to just flick a switch in your mind and turn it from negative to positive in an instant?

All you need to do is make the decision right now to be happy. Once you make that decision think of 1 happy thing. This single happy thought will lead to more and more happy thoughts.

If you do find that a negative thought creeps in be aware of it and stop your thoughts immediately. Imagine that your thoughts are like a book; now flip back a few pages to that negative thought. Rip out the page in your mind and crumple it up. Drop it on the ground and in real life take your foot and squish it into the ground. Strongly say to yourself that you will never think about that negative thought ever again.

When using this technique you may feel foolish by squishing things into the ground that don't physically exist but this technique works and you will find yourself doing this less and less as those negative thoughts are replaced with positive ones.

By maintaining a constant happy mood you will notice over time that your work is progressing at an ever increasing pace.

Gratitude

The importance of feeling gratitude on a daily basis cannot be emphasised enough. When you express gratitude for everything in your life, no matter how small, the Universe will present opportunities to you that will vastly improve your life and make every day feel like a wonderful experience.

Each morning, before you get out of bed, express gratitude for surviving the night because many people on this planet did not survive. Feel the feelings of what it is to be grateful for having another day of life. As you brush your teeth and prepare for the day ahead be grateful for as many things as you can possibly think of.

As you leave the house be grateful for the day, even if it's raining be grateful for the experience of the raindrops hitting your skin. As you go about your day express gratitude to everyone and anyone that does anything for you. Did someone open a door for you today? Did you thank them? You should have. Always thank those who do something for you and give them a smile while you're at it. By thanking someone and smiling at them you are giving away a little bit of happiness. Now it may seem that you should hold onto and horde happiness for yourself but when you give it away the Universe will deliver far more happiness back to you.

Be grateful for how much more productive you are becoming and how better your life has become as a result.

Be grateful that you have now learned new techniques to deal with stress and any failures that come your way.

One of the best ways to express gratitude is to write down a list of things that you are grateful for. Keep a journal and each day, after work; write out 3 things that you feel grateful for. Did you get the big project finished? Did someone unexpectedly help you to get your work completed on time today? Write it all down.

The Universe will always reward those who give away some of their happiness and are grateful for the opportunity to do so. By being grateful you are inviting into your life more and more opportunities to feel grateful, so more and more good things will happen to you as a result.

Focus and Meditation

You can't possibly expect to become more productive if you are unable to focus on the important tasks that need to be completed. Meditation will not only calm your mind but will also greatly enhance your ability to focus for long periods of time.

I know it seems counterintuitive to spend time each day on meditation when you could use that time working, however, if you spend just 10 minutes each morning to meditate you will find that more work is achievable in a shorter period of time so this should easily cancel out any time spent performing this exercise.

There is nothing too complicated involved in meditating and once you perfect the technique you will automatically perform your meditation ritual each morning as if you are on auto pilot.

Find a quiet room and remove, or turn off, all electronic distractions. Do not put your phone on silent or aeroplane mode, instead turn it off, or leave it in another room. Sit on a comfortable chair or lie down and close your eyes. Take deep breaths and focus your mind on your breathing. Feel the oxygen entering your lungs and the harmful carbon dioxide leaving your body. Try to empty your mind of all thoughts and only focus on your breathing. Imagine that when you breathe in that the air inhaled is bright and white, warm and inviting. As you exhale imagine that this carbon dioxide is black and nasty.

In this way, you will be inhaling the good and exhaling the bad. Your subconscious will pick up on this after a few days and will literally believe that you are inhaling good vibes and exhaling all the bad things in your life.

That's it. There is nothing more to meditation. Perform this task for at least

10 minutes each morning, preferably after you have washed and prepared for the day. If performed correctly you will see an immediate increase in your ability to focus on your work from the first day.

Daydream

When was the last time that you got lost in your own thoughts? Isn't it interesting that we only do this when we are approaching the time for a foreign holiday or party event that we are really looking forward to with great anticipation? What if you daydreamed on a daily basis? What would you dream about?

Try to get into the habit of spending at least 15 minutes every day to let your mind wonder. A great place to start is to imagine what your life will be like 10 years from now. It must not be your imagined life based on any current situation, remember that your career, finances and life can change in ways you can't possibly imagine in the blink or an eye. Instead, dream up your version of a perfect life. Think of the giant mansion that you want to live in and all the wonderful things you want to have.

As you begin to build an image of your ideal future life try to focus on the small details. Over time you will be able to construct a very vivid image of every part of this future existence. It will become like a virtual world where you can enter at any point and navigate around your mansion as if you already live there.

Whatever future existence you dream up for yourself make sure that you are very happy with how it all turns out. Get rid of anything from this world that does not make you happy. Who knows, the Universe might deliver this image to reality. Only time will tell.

Cultivate Childlike Curiosity

As a stressful adult it becomes more and more necessary to return to a childlike state of wonder and curiosity. Think about it, when you were a child you were free of all stress and could spend all of your time playing, investigating and learning about new things. Did you know that some of the most successful innovators, inventors and entrepreneurs never lost their childlike wonder?

Everything and anything should begin to become more and more interesting to you as the days go on. Pick one thing to be curious about before you go to work in the morning. Maybe you see a colony of ants scurrying across the driveway outside your house. Crouch down close to them and begin to think about this group of ants. Where are they going? What will they do when they get there? Where is their base? See if you can track them back to where they live. Don't get any bright ideas about killing them; they are your great wonder for the day after all.

The ants were your push. It is up to you to discover more and more things to be curious about and it is **you** who must dream up of more things to wonder about. Try to find at least 3 things to fill your cognitive power with. These 3 things should be completely unrelated to work, such as those ants in the driveway.

See it as Already Finished

One of the biggest barriers to productivity is the constant and never ending pile of work that your boss presents to you each morning. You know this will never end and every day will be the exact same, more and more work. This nags at your subconscious mind to solidify the monotonous existence that you find yourself in.

This way of thinking is no different to when you stub your toe on the bed in the morning. When this happens your day will usually turn into a complete disaster because you focused on the bad luck that struck you as you got out of bed. Because you gave your focus to the negative you continued to receive reasons to be negative throughout the day. If you continually focus on the never-ending pile of work and a monotonous existence then that is exactly what the Universe will give you, more reasons to have a monotonous existence.

To change this subconscious programming it is important to focus on already having your daily work completed before you even begin work. You could spend the drive to work focusing on how great it feels to have completed your days' work so quickly. Imagine that the pile of paperwork is complete and already stacked neatly in the "*out*" box or that the architectural model you are working on is already complete and looking fantastic. Whatever you do for a living it is vital that you imagine those tasks as fully complete, very early in the day. Who knows, your boss might give you the rest of the day off for doing such good work.

The most important aspect of imagining your day of work as already finished is to be happy about it. How fantastic would it feel to actually have it all done? How fantastic would it feel to be allowed to go home early today, especially on such a fine sunny day? Cultivate a feeling of happiness and the Universe can't help but sit up and take notice. Every molecule and atom in this existence will begin to move in directions that will ultimately bring your imagined reality into existence.

The Importance of Sleep

"Sleep is the best meditation."
                    Dalai Lama (b. 1950)

Did you know that a lack of good quality sleep over an extended period of time can, and usually does, lead to premature death? The worst part is not the premature death but the detrimental health and performance effects that you will suffer from until you die. It is impossible to perform any task to its full potential if you are suffering from sleep deprivation.

Chronic sleep deprivation can lead to:

- Decreased alertness
- Memory impairment
- Depression
- An overall poor quality of life
- Fetal retardation (in pregnant women)
- Stress

- High blood pressure
- Stroke
- Heart failure

If you are getting less than 6 hours of sleep per night on a regular basis you are putting yourself at increased risk of suffering from the symptoms listed above. If you have been depriving yourself of valuable sleep over any period of time than your body may have acclimatised itself and you will need to re-train your body to accept a few more hours of sleep per night.

One of the best ways to ensure that you fall asleep is to turn off all electronics at least 2 hours before bedtime. These devices are constantly stimulating your brain to remain in a wakeful state rendering proper sleep impossible.

If you routinely fall asleep by watching TV in your bedroom what is actually happening is that your brain has become accustomed to drifting into a sleep state but that TV is actually keeping your subconscious in a constant state of alertness. This means that, although you may sleep you are not getting the proper quality of sleep that you should be getting.

Think about your waking routine. Do you jump out of bed in the morning feeling energised and having a strong lust for life and the day ahead, or do you literally drag yourself begrudgingly out of bed and force yourself to get ready for the terrible day ahead? If you are filled with energy and jump out of bed in the morning it means you are getting enough good quality sleep. If, however, your morning routine is a struggle than you are putting yourself into a state of chronic sleep deprivation.

Turning off all electronics 2 hours before bedtime is just one of the methods of getting an early night without resorting to sleeping pills or tranquillizers. Another method is to have a cup of hot chamomile tea approximately

1 hour before bedtime and spend the last hour reading a book. Not an electronic device or eReader but an actual paper book. Do not read this book while lying in bed, as we are trying to associate the act of lying in bed with sleeping.

Eventually, you will retrain your brain to drift into a deep sleep the moment your head hits the pillow.

The Resting Paradox

It is very likely that you are reading this book because you are stressed out and working so much that it might seem at times that there aren't enough hours in the day to get your work done, let alone get some time to sleep.

If you have been putting the points in this book into practice you will have only added more work to your already busy day, but hopefully, by now, you are beginning to see dramatic benefits and an increase in productivity. That boost in productivity can now be turbocharged by getting good quality sleep and rest when necessary.

When you think of Einstein do you think of a man spending 18 hours per day writing on a blackboard trying to come up with answers? You may be surprised to know that Einstein not only got a lengthy nightly sleep but used to take frequent naps during the day.

It is common to encounter obstacles and blocks to projects or tasks that you are trying to accomplish and most people will continue working and getting stressed trying to find the solution. If you encounter such a situation in your working life it is important to step back immediately and leave the area. In your mind ask the Universe for the solution to your particular problem and feel happy that you are going to get the answer you need. Now either enjoy a restful time in a nearby park or have a relaxing stroll around the block or even find a comfy chair in a quiet room and nap for 20 minutes. By the time you get back to the office the solution will have presented itself.

When I was in university there was a young guy in our course who used to sleep a lot. Literally, in every class, this guy would nod off yet he would always attain an A grade in each and every exam. As he napped in class his subconscious mind would soak up the lesson like a sponge while the rest of us were struggling to understand what was being presented to us.

Never underestimate a well-rested subconscious.

Never overwork the problem, always rest and forget about the problem. This is the Universe's strange way of delivering the answers we need.

Slow Down and Relax

In today's hectic world with its instant gratification culture it seems like we need to do our entire life's work right now. This way of thinking will lead to nothing being done as your brain will go into overload and simply give up. Remember that in our working life there will always be work that needs to be done. People have a tendency to become fearful that if you do not perform your work as fast as the next guy that you will either be replaced or you will be held back from promotion. In most countries, promotions don't actually have anything to do with productivity and have more to do with who you know, luck and timing.

How often have you seen the laziest people in your place of employment rising through the ranks like they were being fired into space on the back of a rocket? We are generally conditioned that by doing a lot of work you will get promoted, however, it is the person who does all the work that will remain in that position ...

because they do all the work. Why would they be promoted? Their replacement might not do all the work and somebody has to.

Promotions are not important in this life. Money is not important in this life. Status is not important in this life. The most important thing in this life is you and the experiences you have. While holding down a job and getting a regular wage is necessary, they are only necessary in order for you to enjoy experiences in life, such as meeting friends for a few drinks or going on a foreign holiday to see the sights.

Take plenty of time each day to just sit back and relax.

Are You Rich or Wealthy?

"Wealth consists not in having great possessions, but in having few wants."
　　　　　　　Epictetus (c. 55 – 135 AD)

What's the difference between being rich and being wealthy? When you are rich you have a very well-paying job and money is flowing into your bank account on a constant basis. This richness does not constitute wealth as you may be spending as much as you earn or even more than you earn on a monthly basis. Most people on Earth are only 1 paycheck away from being homeless.

It is important to account for your finances in a way that ensures that if the supply of income was to stop in the morning that you are able to survive for a long period of time. Wealth is not measured by an amount of money but by an amount of time. When someone is 1 year wealthy it means that if the money supply ends they have enough saved to survive for 1 year while maintaining their current expenditure. They are able to make their current rent or mortgage payments each month and enjoy the social activities they enjoy now.

How wealthy are you? Calculate the amount of money you spend each month and divide your savings by this amount. Account for every possible expense. Most people will neglect things like parking fees and sundry items they buy on a daily basis. Doing this calculation may give you a big shock but it is necessary in order for you to realise that saving is extremely important. Some people like to invest their money, however; as we have seen from the economic crash of 2008, these investments can vanish in an instant, so exclude any such investments from your calculations. Also, exclude the value of any property you own as you do not have that money in your bank account. Consider only that money which you can physically withdraw.

So, how wealthy are you? It might be time to downsize that car or cancel your cable subscription. Being wealthy will give you an enormous sense of freedom and serenity. This, in turn, will allow you to focus more intensely on tasks that must be completed. By becoming wealthier it will also free your unconscious mind of this burden which will lead to better sleep and an overall better mood. A good measure of wealth is being able to survive for 1 year if your income stream should stop in the morning.

Keeping up with the Jones's

By viewing your neighbours or friends possessions with envious eyes you are dooming yourself to financial ruin. Most people get themselves into trouble because they feel pressured by society to have certain things and that the price tag associated with those things are some form of measure of social standing. This is a false perception that has been generated by a large-scale and brutal propaganda machine known as advertising.

Advertising exists everywhere and it is impossible to avoid. Even if you believe that you are able to consciously ignore all advertising there is one part of your brain that will constantly soak up all of that input like a sponge ... your subconscious mind.

Advertising is not new and has been carefully honed over a long period of time to elicit certain feelings in the person viewing it. By design, it will suck you into its trap.

You may also have been given the impression that because of your current title (manager, CEO, etc.) that you must drive a certain size car or wear certain, highly expensive, clothes. This is also a societal falsehood. None of these things can ever affect your title or status unless you allow them too. What others think of you is their problem and not yours.

Stop buying highly expensive things in order to keep up with the Jones's or you will eventually come to realise that this race is unwinnable. Only buy items that you actually want or need because if things should ever fall apart for you financially, those same neighbours and colleagues will, most likely, not come to your aid.

Conclusion

Congratulations. You should now feel much better, rested, healthier, happier and productive.

Take a moment to think back on the times before you implemented the techniques outlined in this book. Look at how stressful life used to be. If you are still stuck in those chronically stressful times than you need to re-read this book and follow all the techniques mentioned until you are able to return to this section and realise that the worst is now behind you.

I wish you all the best for your future and hope that it will be the most productive one possible.

About Tadhg O'Flaherty

As a computer whizz-kid, Tadhg was naturally inept at writing until he discovered that by utilising the Law of Attraction he was able to seamlessly transition into the field and is now a full-time author with several books currently self-published on Amazon.

Tadhg's second book "Surviving a Realistic Zombie Apocalypse" gained local notoriety within days of publishing and was featured on the front page of the Limerick Leader newspaper, which has a readership of 110,290 and also received airtime on local and national radio.

To find out more, visit Tadhg's website and sign up to the author's mailing list for advanced notice of new releases, promotions and more.

www.tadhgfla.com

Author's Note

Thank you for reading **Living a Productive Life**. I hope you enjoyed this book. Word-of-mouth is vital for the success of any author. Please consider leaving a review on Amazon. Each review makes all the difference and would be greatly appreciated.

I wish you all the best for the future and **know** that you will thrive in everything you do. What would you do if you knew you couldn't fail ever again? Go and do it, build the life that you want.

Also by Tadhg O'Flaherty

How to Get Over Her in 1 Month: Learn how to rise like a Phoenix from the ashes of a breakup

Surviving a Realistic Zombie Apocalypse

Prepper's: The Ultimate Guide

Living Off-Grid

Living a Happy Life

Do You Really Exist?

How to Reprogram Your Subconscious

Surviving Crippling Poverty

www.ingramcontent.com/pod-product-compliance
Lightning Source LLC
Chambersburg PA
CBHW021017180526
45163CB00005B/1988